Amsterdam in 3 Days:

❧ ❧ ❧

**The Definitive Tourist Guide Book That Helps
You Travel Smart and Save Time**

Book Description

Why should you choose **Amsterdam in 3 Days** for your short-term trip?

This guide is so easy to read, and it's packed with information that you'll find valuable. Sure, you could just follow the other tourists once you arrive, but if you want to ensure that you see all the attractions important to you, they may not be the same places everyone else is headed. We'll help you decide before you arrive which places you want to be sure you see, and which can be added on if your short stay permits.

Using this guide for your trip is the smarter way to travel. We only list high-rated hotels and restaurants in three price ranges, so you can choose the best for you.

This guide is the perfect choice if you've never before visited Amsterdam. We give you the information you'll need to get to town from the airport, and then around town, once you're there.

You'll likely enjoy going over our restaurant section, too – it's split by price points and offers various types of cuisine. Amsterdam has a rich French heritage, so many of the best restaurants do serve French cuisine, but with locally sourced produce.

If you only have several days to spend in Amsterdam, this guide is your perfect choice. Plan and enjoy your trip with the most accurate information at your fingertips.

The People of Amsterdam

The population in Amsterdam's city limits was over 800,000 in 2016. However, counting the suburban areas, the population has been estimated to be 1.1 million people.

Amsterdam has long been famous for its easy-going attitude, and it's not just the marijuana that causes it. They're a laid-back and welcoming people. Amsterdam's historical sites, cannabis shops and red-light district draw in more than five million visitors every year.

Amsterdam's population is almost 50% Dutch, with the remainder of foreign ancestry. Non-Western peoples make up about 35% of the population, and they largely live in separate areas, like Amsterdam-Noord, Zeeburg, Bijlmer and Niew-West. More than 175 nationalities are represented in Amsterdam, ranking it highly in any list of diverse world cities.

Language

Dutch is the official language of Amsterdam, and the rest of the Netherlands, as well. Most residents of Amsterdam speak English fairly well, and many are fluent in one to two other languages, as well. You don't need to learn Dutch to enjoy Amsterdam, but they appreciate it if you try.

Holidays

Jan 1	New Year's Day
April	Good Friday (not an official public holiday)
April	Easter Sunday
April	Easter Monday
April	King's Day
May 4	National Remembrance Day (not an official public holiday)
May 5	Liberation Day (official public holiday only observed every 5 years)
May	Ascension Day
June	Pentecost Sunday (Whitsunday)
June	Pentecost Monday
December	Sinterklaas (not an official public holiday)

December 25	Christmas Day
December 26	Boxing Day
December 31	New Year's Eve (not an official public holiday)

Religious Beliefs

Christianity was the predominant religion of the Netherlands until late in the 1900s. The city is religiously diverse now, but people do not adhere to religion as they did in the past.

34% of the population of the Netherlands identified themselves as Christians in 2006. This has decreased, and in 2015 the percentage was down to 25%. 5% are Muslim and 2% are Buddhists or Hindus.

Many Dutch people believe that religion should not play a role in education or politics. It is seen as a personal matter, and not necessarily practiced in public. Freedom of education for people of all religions is guaranteed in the Dutch constitution. All schools receive funding from the government, regardless of their religious affiliation.

Here is a quick preview of what you will learn in this tourist guide:

- Helpful information about Amsterdam
- Flying into the city
- Transportation tips in town
- Why Amsterdam is such a vibrant tourist spot and what you will find most remarkable about it
- Information on luxury and budget accommodations and what you'll get for your money
- The currency used in Amsterdam
- Tourist attractions you should make time to see
- Other attractions for entertainment and culture

- Events that may be running during your stay

- Tips on the best places to eat & drink for all price points, whether you want simple fare, worldwide dishes or Dutch flavor

Table of Contents

≪≪ ≪

1. Introduction

໔ ໔ ໔

Amsterdam is prosperous, open-hearted and welcoming. The people enjoy their visitors, their boat-folk, cyclists and their own multicultural community. They are approachable, friendly and virtually unflappable. The city is confident of itself, but looks optimistically toward the future.

Amsterdam has many facets in its architecture. It boasts 1280 bridges, over 160 waterways, and mansions from the 1600s sitting beside the Red-Light District's sleazy alleys. It's a city of contrasts, too. It has impressive museums, while still tolerating smoking pot and sex clubs. It has Michelin-Star restaurants in the same area as grungy cafes.

Amsterdam is not a new Sodom and Gomorrah. They are very tolerant, but only to a point. Today, the city is trying to improve the life of its people by closing down some infamous prostitutes' windows and drug haunts. You can now find upmarket stores and restaurants on the side streets of the Red-Light District, and the area is becoming more suitable for travelers.

A Brief History of Amsterdam

Amsterdam began its life in the 1200s as a tiny fishing village. Trade has been its driving force since that time. By the 1600s, beer and other products like diamonds, tobacco, guns and wheat had turned the city into the richest on earth.

In the same time period, the Dutch began their war for independence against the rule of Spain. It was an 80-year war, led by William of Orange, a noble citizen. In 1648, their freedom had been won, and the Netherlands became the only republic found in Western Europe.

The 1600s are also referred to as the Golden Age in the Netherlands, due to Amsterdam's flourishing. Artists of the caliber of Rembrandt led an Amsterdam cultural renaissance and Dutch ships sailed the world, at the same time bringing back valuable and exotic products like silk and spices.

Immigrants have always sought a new life in Amsterdam, often because they were fleeing from persecution by governments in their homelands. The success of Amsterdam has repeatedly been based on cooperation in trade, and on tolerance.

1672 signaled the end of their Golden Age. The Netherlands was attacked by two German States, in addition to France and England.

In 1795, Napoleon and France invaded the Netherlands again. They stayed for almost 20 years, bringing French influence to the Dutch culture and language. After they left in 1813, the Dutch went from a republic to a constitutional monarchy, which it still is today.

The Nazis invaded the country in 1940. Even though the Dutch stayed neutral during World War I, and wished to do the same in World War II, Hitler's army occupied the Netherlands for five years. The impact was immeasurable. The Netherlands would lose more Jewish citizens than another other country occupied by the Nazis. 10% of the population of Amsterdam was lost.

Amsterdam changed greatly in the 60 years that followed WWII. It changed from a trade city into a city based on services. In addition, the fascism they experienced in WW II resulted in more liberal-minded people.

The city became well-known, too, for its tolerating of soft drug use. That is still where they stand today. In addition, the Dutch combined it with their innate business sense, turning cannabis into a prospering industry.

Neighborhoods

The Red Light District

De Wallen, as the Dutch call the Red-Light District, is a must-see for adult tourists in Amsterdam. There is so much more to the area than its saucy aspects, including the largest Buddhist temple in Europe, Amsterdam's Chinatown, picturesque canals and historic landmarks. Even though the better-known aspects of the neighborhood draw some people in, this district is still fascinating and safe.

Eastern Amsterdam/Plantage

In this district, you can tour the historic home of Rembrandt, shop in their huge flea market, or enjoy a craft beer next to the tallest of Dutch wooden windmills. This area is also home to Hortus Botanicus, which is among the oldest of the world's botanical gardens, and the Artis Royal Zoo, which is lovely and very well-kept.

Museum Quarter (Museumkwartier)

Visitors come to this area to visit the Van Gogh Museum and Rijksmuseum, among others. If you need a short break from museums, check out the largest park in Amsterdam – Vondelpark - and the Concertgebouw music hall.

You may also enjoy the high-end shopping available in this neighborhood. And during evening time, the Museum Quarter takes on another life, as a quiet and calm oasis.

Jordaan, Amsterdam

Jordaan is home to some of Amsterdam's favorite bars and one of their favorite outdoor markets. The narrow streets offer peeks into quality galleries and quirky shops. Traditionally, this neighborhood was an immigrant and working-class haven; it's now better-known for designers and artists. There are many locals who stop by for a drink and shopping, too, so it's not just a tourist attraction.

Eastern Docklands

Architectural masterpieces including the Python Bridge and Openbare Bibiotheek, and the scenic waterfront, bring tourists to this area. It offers trendy clubs, bars, restaurants and cafes. There are cool galleries to enjoy, the National Maritime Museum and a kid-friendly attraction in Science Center NEMO.

De Pijp

De Pijp is home to the most famous and largest outdoor market in Amsterdam. Beyond the busy main street, smaller lanes beckon you to explore its hidden gems. Almost 50% of the residents here are foreigners, and many are students. The area also offers great bars, restaurants and cafes and many locally owned stores.

Centrum

This is the hub of Amsterdam, home to its tram network hub and many commuters and tourists. It's an excellent starting place for the best of street life, sightseeing and shopping. You're also quite close to Haalremmerdijt's shops and the Royal Palace. Dam Square and the Red Light Districts are easily accessible from this area, as is the Canal Ring.

Canal Ring

This is a UNESCO World Heritage Site, and as popular as it is historic. Whether you're a shutterbug or history buff, you'll find plenty worth looking into while you wander here. Major tourist attractions in the area include Grachtengordel's bridges and canals, De Negen Straatjes' independent boutiques and the floating flower market of Bloemenmarkt.

What does Amsterdam offer its Visitors?

Amsterdam is a vibrant city. From the historical buildings to museums and canals, it is one of the most beautiful and romantic of

European cities. You can see a lot of the city with a canal cruise, which can be much more relaxing than mass transit.

Amsterdam speaks of diversity and tolerance. It has all the things you could want from a large city, with its public transport, international restaurants and lively nightlife. But, due to the use of its canal system, it doesn't have much road traffic.

Most people spend time at the museums while they're in Amsterdam. There are more than 70 museums, attracting millions of tourists every year. There is sure to be one – or more – that will be of interest to you.

2. Key Information about Amsterdam

❧ ❧ ❧

Money Matters

The official currency of the Netherlands is the Euro. This will make things very easy to get around in a relaxed way, especially if you're from a Western European country. Otherwise, you can exchange money in any bank in Amsterdam.

There are also ATMs in many public places. You can use them to withdraw money directly in euros. However, keep in mind that certain banks charge fairly high fees for international transactions. Ideally, you should exchange money.

Alternately, you can also use a credit or debit card such as Visa, Mastercard, or American Express. These types of card are widely accepted around Amsterdam in malls, restaurants, travel points, or hotels, especially in very central parts of the city.

Tipping

As is the case in many European cities, tipping is not really expected. Some services will have a service charge already on the bill. You can always leave some extra change or round up your total in cafes, restaurants and bars. There is no need to tip higher unless you really got great service.

Restaurant Tipping

Tipping is only expected in Netherlands restaurants if you have good or even exceptional service. Tipping is usually figured at 5 to 10% of your bill. Give your service person the tip yourself.

Hotel Tipping

Tipping is not expected in Amsterdam, unless you stay for a long time, or if you receive extra services. Even if you do, the tipping (or not) is still up to you. Some hotels add a 15% service charge on your bill. People usually tip porters 1-2 Euros for each bag.

3. Transport to and in Amsterdam

❧ ❧ ❧

Getting to Amsterdam by Plane

Schiphol Amsterdam Airport is the main airport used for international flights in the Netherlands and Holland. It is found about six miles from the center of Amsterdam. It is often simply called "Schiphol".

Getting to the City from the Airport

The Dutch national train operations company, Nederlandse Spoorwegen (abbreviated as NS), runs a passenger rail station under the passenger terminal at the airport. They offer 24 hour a day transportation to Amsterdam, as well as into Rotterdam, Utrecht and The Hague.

Schiphol is also easy to access by bus. Many buses stop at the station located in front of the terminal.

Amsterdam Rental Cars

You can pick up a car at the Car Rental & Service Desk. You'll find it in the main foyer of the airport. Many major car rental companies offer service at Schiphol, including Enterprise, Sixt, Europcar, Avis, Alamo and Hertz. You don't need a car to experience Amsterdam. There are many pedestrian-only areas in the city.

Amsterdam Cabs

Taxis are a comfortable way to get from the airport into the center of Amsterdam. Various companies have taxi service from the airport. A trip to Amsterdam from Schiphol is a flat

$47 USD. If you reserve one online, the cost may be as high as $59 USD.

The ranks of taxis can be found outside the arrival hall at the airport. It takes about 15 minutes to get into the city, although peak hours may lead to a longer trip. Use official Amsterdam airport taxis, since they are more closely regulated, and safer.

You can't hail taxis on the streets in Amsterdam. When you want to catch a cab, head for the taxi lines, found in designated areas. From restaurants or hotels, the employees can call you a cab.

Payment and Tipping for Taxi's

The fare for taxis in Amsterdam:

Taxi (standard car – holds 4 people) – start tariff is $3.55 USD

The price per kilometer is $2.61 USD
Price for each minute waiting in traffic is 43 cents USD

It's not common for people to tip their taxi drivers in Amsterdam, but if you like, you can leave a Euro or two, or round up your bill.

Public Transport in Amsterdam

Using public transportation to travel in Amsterdam is convenient and straightforward. The city's neighborhoods are connected by bus, ferry, metro, tram and train.

Depending on your length of stay and travel plans, there are various passes that may work for you.

Passes & Tickets

The "I amsterdam" City Card offers free entrance to some of Amsterdam's favorite attractions, and unlimited use of the public transport system for 24, 48 or 72 hours. The 72-hour pass works exceptionally well for a three-day visit.

You can purchase passes discounted online, or buy from one of the places listed below, when you arrive. The prices vary according to discount offered, but $70 USD is typical for a three-day pass.

Remember, this pass is not just for transport. It will also get you into 38 local museums FREE, including the Hermitage Amsterdam, the Rembrandthuis Museum and the Van Gogh Museum.

If you don't order your pass online, there are many places you can purchase one. They include:

- Amsterdam Central Station
- Amsterdam Airport Schiphol - I amsterdam Visitor Centre
- Connexxion Help Desk, Arrival Hall 4 (behind Starbucks)
- Amsterdam Central Station
- I amsterdam Visitor Centre at Stationsplein
- Amsterdam Public Library
- Museumplein
- Waterlooplein
- Bijlmer ArenA Station
- Amsterdam Lelylaan Station
- Amsterdam Zuid Station
- Zeeburg
- Most Shell petrol stations
- All Canal shop locations

4. Accommodations

ๅๆ ๅๆ ๅๆ

Amsterdam is a tourist city, accustomed to laying out the best for her guests. Whether you want to be pampered in luxury, or just desire a place to lay your head at the end of the day, Amsterdam has you covered.

Because not all of the areas and attractions are generally listed in Dutch, we will list them here, along with their translation:

- Begijnhof - old inner court in Amsterdam
- Leidseplein – a busy square in Canal Ring
- Rijksmuseum – The Museum of the Netherlands

- Stopera – building that houses city Hall & Dutch National Opera and Ballet
- Hortus Botanicus – Botanical Gardens of Amsterdam
- Westerkerk – Reformed Church in central Amsterdam

Prices for Luxury Hotels: $600 USD per night and up

Canal House Suites at Sofitel Legend The Grand Amsterdam
- Close to The Old Church, City Center, Amsterdam Museum, New Church, Royal Palace, Dam Square

Dream Hotel Amsterdam
- Close to Flower Market, Canal Ring, Skinny Bridge, Begijnhof, Amsterdam Museum, Rembrandt Square

Amsterdam Downtown Hotel

- Close to Leidseplein, Canal Ring, Rembrandt Square, Amsterdam Museum, Begijnhof, Flower Market

Prices for Mid-Range Hotels: $300 USD to $500 USD per night

Conservatorium Hotel

- Close to Stedelijk Museum, Museum Quarter, Leidseplein, Rijksmuseum, Van Gogh Museum, Concertgebouw

Intercontinental Amstel Amsterdam

- Close to Skinny Bridge, Canal Ring, Rembrandt Square, Hortus Botanicus, Heineken Experience, Stopera

Pulitzer Amsterdam

- Close to Anne Frank House, Canal Ring, Amsterdam Museum, Dam Square, New Church, Royal Palace

Prices for Least Expensive Hotels: $100 USD and less

Tropen Hotel Amsterdam

- Close to NEMO Science Museum, Skinny Bridge, National Maritime Museum, Artis, Hortus Botanicus

Hotel Atlas Vondelpark

- Close to Stedelijk Museum, Museum Quarter, Leidseplein, Rijksmuseum, Van Gogh Museum, Concertgebouw

The Muse Amsterdam Boutique Hotel

- Close to Concertgebouw, Museum Quarter, Heineken Experience, Van Gogh Museum, Stedelijk Museum, Rijksmuseum

Airbnb's

The average price for an Airbnb in Rome is $141 USD per night. This includes everything from single private rooms to large estates, suitable for groups.

Price range:

- $12 USD per night for a simple room with one bed and a shared bathroom
- $59 to $189 USD per night for a deluxe apartment with a private bathroom
- $467+ USD per night for a comfortable luxury condo with all the amenities

5. Sightseeing

❧ ❧ ❧

There is so much to do in Amsterdam. Much of it is historical sites and in museums, but that isn't all the city has to offer. We're giving you many historic places from which to choose, and some experiences that are simply fun. You'll learn a lot about the country and the city.

Anne Frank Museum

This museum has been dedicated to the life of Anne Frank, which was cut short by the Nazis. She is among the best known of the Holocaust victims. In the home where she and her family lived for a lot of WW II, you can almost see the place where they hid from the Nazis.

In this house, now a museum, Anne wrote her diary, which would become a best-seller after the end of the war. Sadly, she died just two months before the war was over. A good deal of the home is the same as it was in her time. This makes it an even more poignant reminder of this tragic era of history.

The Rijksmuseum

This is a popular attraction in Amsterdam, and its most important repository of art. It was founded back in 1809, so that the Netherlands had a proper place to house their antiquities and rare art collections. Today, this includes about seven million art works, and the museum also boasts 35,000 manuscripts and books, and displays that deal with the development of culture and art in the country.

The Royal Palace

This building once served as the Town Hall. Now it is the residence of the King, when he is in Amsterdam. The structure is supported by over 13,000 pilings, sunk in 1648, when construction began. The architecture is an homage to that of Rome, with a classical exterior and a magnificent interior.

The apartments in the Royal Palace are decorated with many friezes, reliefs, ornamentation and marble sculptures. Its highlights also include a collection of fine furniture, some of the finest seen anywhere in the world. The Council Hall is the most important of rooms, and also the largest. It is decorated sumptuously, and has been called one of the loveliest staterooms of Europe. You can ask about guided tours in English, too.

The Begijnhof

This is a tranquil spot in the inner city, which is a rarity in Amsterdam. If you hurry past, you might not even notice it. Many of the older homes in the area are still occupied, but the pathways and tiny lanes around the building provide access to the area. These are some of Amsterdam's oldest houses, with their well-kept courtyards of green. The area was occupied originally by a Catholic commune, and the small chapel in the area, in which services are still held, only saw the last of the women buried in 1971.

Kalverstraat and Vlooienmarkt

Here is a place to rest your brain from history studies, and enjoy some shopping. This is the busiest shopping area, and the most well-known. It holds souvenirs and local crafts, as well as high-end luxury goods. Kalverstraat is also home to restaurants, cafes, galleries and smaller sized boutiques.

Vlooienmarkt is a different type of shopping experience. It's the most famous of Amsterdam's flea markets, in business since 1886. There are so many types of goods you can find here, from food and antiques to new and used clothing.

6. Eat & Drink

1.

2. ◆ ◆ ◆

3.

Traditional Dutch cuisine is fairly straightforward and simple. They use little meat, but a great emphasis is placed on vegetables. Their breakfasts and lunches usually consist of bread and toppings, and dinner is mainly meat & potatoes, with seasonal vegetables.

Fine Dining Restaurants - $$$$

Brasserie Ambassade - $$$$

Brasserie Ambassade places an emphasis on local, artisan, seasonal and fresh products. The French dishes served here are classic and delicious. Among the favorites are rillettes of duck, with cornichons, brioche bread and picked onions. Also popular is their baked duck liver with plum compote.

de Silveren Spiegel - $$$$

The tasting menu at this restaurant has many inspired choices, which will allow you to get a true taste of the local produce, in delicate dishes. Try the Zeeland mussels with monkfish, celeriac and cantharelles, with foamy, mild anise sauce. Another favorite is their glazed lamb neck with pearl barley and parsnips.

Envy - $$$$

The goal of Envy is for you to taste pure products and fine ingredients. Some of their dishes are simple and others have a gourmet touch. You'll have many surprises along the way. Envy doesn't have a standard menu. You won't see starters and main courses. Rather, they serve surprising, small dishes that you are welcome to taste and share. The chefs will be happy to work their magic on local, seasonal produce, to entice your taste buds.

Midrange Restaurants - $$ - $$$

Guts and Glory - $$-$$$

This is a stripped-down and lively eatery near Rembrandt Square. It's among the most popular of all the places to eat in Amsterdam, and there are a lot of them. They serve Italian dishes, and their signature dish has a one-ingredient menu they call "chapter". It changes every few months, and includes vegetarian, pork, beef, fish and chicken dishes.

Nam Kee - $$$

Although many restaurants in Amsterdam serve French dishes, you can get some wonderful Chinese food, too. Nam Kee is most well-known for their Peking duck display in the window. Try their steamed oysters in simple black bean sauce, for an unadorned treat that is difficult to top.

Le Garage - $$$

Le Garage was named because the building housing it was once a mechanic shop. It was opened in 1990. Celebrities can be seen often, and the décor has not changed from the black and red of their original opening. There is much French influence in their dishes, like their steak tartare, but they also serve some modern dishes, like tuna pizza and squid carbonara.

Cheap Eats - $

Broodjeszaak 't Kuyltje - $

The Dutch don't always make time for leisurely lunches, but they do like to grab good sandwiches to go. This is one of the places that offers that taste. There are lines during lunch time for their pastrami sandwiches. They are also well-known for their Tartaar Special, which includes hardboiled egg, onion and minced raw beef.

Haringstal Ab Kromhout - $

Dutch herring is often believed to be raw, but it is actually salt-cured. While herring food stalls are common, Haringstal Ab Kromhout comes highly recommended. You can order natural herring or get it topped with pickle and chopped raw onion.

FEBO - $

Deep-fried snacks are famous in Amsterdam, and this 75-years-young fast food restaurant offers deep fried bitterballen and kroket. You might wish to try their frikandel, too – it's a typical kind of sausage. Deep fried cheese pockets are also very popular, and this chain of restaurants offers these and other deep fried treats all over the city.

7. Culture and Entertainment

✿ ✿ ✿

Amsterdam has a diverse culture and architecture. It's a harbor city, and is thus linked to many other countries. Art galleries and museums are many and varied, and their festivals are quite popular with international visitors. Ballet, theater and opera admirers will enjoy the performances staged here. You can find nearly any type of entertainment in Amsterdam.

The West Church

Also known as Westerkerk, this is one of the most visited churches in the city. Although its architecture is primarily Renaissance style, it has many external and internal features that are undeniably Gothic in style. Its 279-foot tower, called "Tall John", is the tallest in Amsterdam.

Within the tower, the hours are marked by a carillon. Its 48 bells are of various sizes, the largest being 3.25 tons. Some other of the church's highlights are a 1622 organ, a 1905 marble column and the interred remains of Rembrandt.

Van Gogh Museum

Vincent Van Gogh captured imagination like no other artists of the 1800s. 1.5 million people visit this museum yearly. It is widely thought of as one of the most important art galleries in the world. It was opened in 1973, and boasts the largest collection of Van Gogh's work in the world. This includes 200+ paintings, 700 letters and 500+ drawings.

Rembrandt House Museum

Rembrandt and his wife spent the most successful, happiest years of his life in his

Amsterdam house that is now the Rembrandt House Museum. This is where he found the models for his works of Biblical art, and painted sights he saw from outings along Amsterdam's canals. Rembrandt lived in the house for about 20 years. It is furnished in 1600s style.

The Stedelijk: Amsterdam's Municipal Museum

The Stedelijk Museum houses one of the most impressive collections of modern art in Europe. It focuses on 1800s and 1900s French and Dutch paintings. Their works include art from Warhol (pop art) and Matisse. They also have a sculpture garden containing works by Renoir, Rodin and others.

The Jewish Historical Museum

This museum is housed between four different synagogues, the oldest dating back to the year 1670. Its highlights include religious artifacts like Torah headdresses and robes. They also display ceremonial canopies and hangings.

A library is found in the Jewish Historical Museum, and a kosher restaurant is located in the Upper Synagogue. The Docker Monument was erected to commemorate a workers' strike in 1941, when the workers refused to assist in deporting Jewish citizens of Amsterdam.

Botanical Gardens and Zoo

In Amsterdam's heart are two marvels of natural beauty. The Botanical Gardens is one of the oldest in the world, opened in 1638. It started out as a simple herb garden for apothecaries and doctors, it now boasts exotic flowers, rare trees and other plants and a large greenhouse with tropical plants.

Just a few minute's walk from the Botanical gardens is Artis, the popular Amsterdam zoo. It houses animals and other creatures from many areas of the world. Historic buildings also dot the zoo path.

The aquarium teaches about coral reefs and the inside makings of the type of canal found in Amsterdam. They also offer a butterfly pavilion, an insectarium, a zoological museum, a house for nocturnal animals and even a planetarium.

Amsterdam Night-Life

Amsterdam at night is totally different from the city you see during the day. Some people spend evenings strolling along the canals, enjoying the peace. But inside clubs and bars, the city is exciting in a way that doesn't happen in the daylight hours.

There is no one single area in which to experience Amsterdam's night life. The main club areas are Rembrandtplein and Leidseplein, but there are clubs and bars scattered elsewhere in the city, too. There are all kinds of music, and comedy clubs, too. Whatever you're into, Amsterdam will have something to interest you. Here are a few of the favorite clubs.

Paradiso

This club is a haven for creativity, found in a former church. Now a cultural center, concert hall and nightclub, it attracts people in many age groups. Five nights each week, Paradiso functions as a club, giving people a place to dance and let loose. Famous performers, including Lady Gaga and Al Green, have played in the main hall. Lesser known musicians play the Small Hall. Paradiso has the music scene covered in every form, from blues and reggae to country, soul, folk, rock and electric.

Boom Chicago

Entertainment and comedy are on the menu at Boom Chicago. American expats founded the club, and they have a rabid following among lovers of comedy. It's located in the center of town, so you can start or finish your night there. There is a variety of packages that accompany the comedy sets, so you can complete the evening with a canal tour or drinks.

Jimmy Woo

This luxurious club will dazzle you with their design and blow you away with their sound. It has been awarded the having the best club sound in the country. They have themed nights, or you can just relax upstairs with a drink or dance downstairs to the DJ. Each night is unique. The space is cozy, holding only 600 people or so. Be sure to reserve a table or get there early.

8. Special Events in Amsterdam

❧ ❧ ❧

National Tulip Day   January

This is the official launch of Amsterdam's tulip season. They fill Dam Square with about 200,000 tulips. They make a large, temporary garden, open to everyone, even if you want to pick flowers.

CinemAsia Film Festival   March

The CinemAsia festival showcases recent Asian films. They have well-considered sections with six feature films. Film & Food events show films and have food from countries in Asia. They even feature an Asian market.

Amsterdam Wine Festival   March

This festival accents wines from various areas of the world each year. You can taste some specially selected wines, participate in workshops and purchase books that explain wine-making.

Japanese Sakura (Cherry Blossom watching)   April

This is a truly traditional Japanese celebration of cherry trees blossoming. The best place to experience the event is in the Japanese Bloesempark. 400 cherry blossom trees were planted by Japanese expats to memorialize the tsunami that struck Asia in 2004. Families often picnic under the trees.

Koningsdag - King's Day   April

Kings Day is the nation's celebration of the King's birthday, but it's also a good reason to have festive parties all around the Netherlands, particularly in larger cities like Amsterdam. It is a large open-air festival, and almost a million people have shown up to participate in past years.

Remembrance and Liberation Days May

These memorial celebrations are held yearly, to remember the fallen from WWII and the 1945 Liberation of the Netherlands by Allied troops. Liberation Day celebrates democracy and freedom. Some shops will close or shorten their hours. Liberation Day is only celebrated one time every five years. The next is in 2020.

Holland Festival   June

This is Amsterdam's largest artistic festival, with participants from all over the world. It covers fields that include dance, music, opera and theater. It attracts many interesting artistic shows and film screenings, as well.

Taste of Amsterdam   June

This culinary festival runs over a prolonged weekend in June. Amstelpark restaurants serve good food in the park. You'll have a chance to meet some of the city's chefs and even sip a champagne or good wine, while you enjoy the wonderful food.

Grachtenfestival   August

Over 80 jazz and classical music concerts take place during this 10-day festival. They are sometimes enjoyed in gardens and houses of locals, and sometimes in museums, historic buildings, and concert halls. Some concerts are outdoors, too. They take place in the area around Prinsengracht.

Open Monuments Days   September

This is an excellent festival to plan a short vacation around. It offers public admissions to monuments and buildings that are normally inaccessible to the public. They include old factories, ancient farmhouses, castles, palaces and luxury canal houses. In total, over 4,000 monuments in the Netherlands are accessible, free of charge.

Amsterdam Dance Event   October

Amsterdam Dance Event, abbreviated as ADE, just happens to be one of the world leaders in electronic music parties and conferences. Each year, in mid-October, hundreds of thousands flock to Amsterdam for 300 music events held in the city.

Museum Night   November

On one of the first Saturdays in November, the museums in Amsterdam stay open for the whole night. Most of them run special Amsterdam events and programs.

Amsterdam Light Festival   November – January

This festival features a series of light shows and other evening performances, in addition to 40 lit sculptures installed in Amsterdam's Canal Ring. Since the winter days in the Netherlands are shorter, the sculptures allow for attractive evening walks.

Christmas   December

If you're in Amsterdam in the Christmas holiday season, you'll find a variety of festivals and markets that will allow you to incorporate some Danish culture into the holidays.

New Year's Eve   December 31

Amsterdam is wild on New Year's Eve, in a good way. Some families stay home until midnight, so some bars open at that time. The typical club areas in Nieuwmarkt, Rembrandtplein and Leidseplein offer many New Year's Eve parties.

From midnight, you'll stare in wonder as the sky is lit up by the city's fireworks display. Some of the best fireworks shows are found on the bridge that crosses the Bloemgracht and Prinsengracht canals.

9. Safety in Amsterdam

❧ ❧ ❧

Amsterdam is a safe place to visit. In fact, it ranked #5 on the Safe City Index in 2015. You can certainly purchase marijuana easily in coffee shops and smart drugs in shops that specialize in them. In addition, prostitution is legal. However, the city is not dangerous.

The police handle traffic, and since most people bike, there aren't very many traffic jams. In addition, the air is much less polluted than in cities that still rely on cars for their main means of transportation.

Amsterdam is also safe when it comes to crime. The risk for a violent assault is all but absent, in all areas of the city. The general crime rates are still going down each year.

On the other hand, most robberies and pick-pocketing in the city are perpetrated on tourists. They are more targeted than residents because they're easier to distract. You should be aware of people coming too close to you, especially in tourist areas. Thieves know that tourists usually carry more cash than locals do.

To avoid being a victim of pickpocketing:

- Don't use a large wallet and don't carry a lot of money if you don't need it.
- Keep your purse or bag closed, and held close to your body.
- Don't leave your wallet or purse unattended on a stroller or cart, or in paid cloak rooms at clubs or bars.

The places with the most incidences of pickpockets in Amsterdam include Damrak, Central Station, Kalverstraat shopping area, and while entering or exiting bars, restaurants, hotel lobbies, metros, trams and buses.

The Red Light District in Amsterdam does have more crime than other areas. However, you won't likely notice it. There are more instances of organized crime, with prostitutes who work for pimps (that is illegal), and money laundering in dodgy coffee shops or dirty sex clubs.

10. Conclusion

෨ ෨ ෨

If you're preparing to take a trip to Amsterdam, this book gives you valuable insight into the best places to stay and the restaurants with the best and most unique foods. We also pointed out the favorite attractions that you may want to see. Don't wait until you get to Amsterdam to decide what you want to see. There are so many amazing places that you need a plan.

We've shown you which attractions are well worth the time, and what areas have the best nightlife, if that interests you. We've opened your eyes to all the best that Amsterdam offers you, so you can plan ahead and relax when you're there, making the most of the short time you have to spend. We've made sure you won't miss anything.